HAUNTED HALLOWEEN

Poetry

Ooooo...Scary

"HAUNTED HALLOWEEN POEMS"

Inspiration on the fly
Published by PoemCatcher Creations
Salisbury Centre
2 Salisbury Road
Edinburgh, EH16 5AB

www.poemcatcher.com

Copyright
All the poems in this book were donated with love and permission to be published. It would be thievery to steal the copyright from the authors. It remains their own.

This is their beautiful creativity and I am just a creative collator.

Cover Design by Trevor at Fresh Digital
Back Cover Photos by Richie Gunn & Aroosha Laghaee

Use of this material is welcomed – providing it inspires, engages and enthrals audiences.

Each and every poem in this book is brilliant. If you disagree, send £10 with your complaint to a child in Haiti.

ISBN978-0-9566018-7-2

This book was made over the Halloween Weekend
and Samhuin festivals on the streets
of Edinburgh, 2010

Its very scary.

About the messy bits...

Think, feel, doodle, make a list, ~~scratch some lines out~~, start again, find more paper, talk to your friends, gather ideas, just look around. They are here to be found.

Many of you did,
believed that you could
You did brilliant
I knew that you would
I love your first efforts
With edits and all
The edge of creation
A little bit raw.

P.S. this book is full of mistakes. Such is life.
Some are mine, some are yours.
I don't mind.
The struggle for perfectionism ain't worth the stress.
I far prefer a creative mess.

£2 per book goes to charity

SOS Children's Villages provides a family for life for children who have lost their parents through war, famine, disease, natural disaster and poverty. Over 78,000 orphaned and abandoned children are cared for by SOS mothers in clusters of family homes in more than 500 of our unique Children's Villages in 124 countries worldwide. Thousands more children benefit from SOS Children's outreach support which includes education, vocational training, medical care and community development programmes. SOS Children also provides emergency relief in situations of crisis and disaster, and continues to support families in earthquake and tsunami-affected countries.

Registered Charity Number 1069204
www.soschildrensvillages.org.uk

CONTENTS

THE PARTY 8
Hatters Halloween 9
Cauldrons 10
Jenny's Halloween 11
Halloween 12
Hallow's Eve 13
My Sh*t Halloween Poem! 14
Halloween House 15
"Surprise" 16
Binary Halloween Haiku 17

PAPARAZZI 18
Flashers 19
Forgot 20
I've seen the PoemCatcher**Error! Bookmark not defined.** 21
Fancy Dress 22
Make Believe on All Hallows Eve 23
October Theifs 24
Zombie Walk 25
Images on Halloween 26
Halloween 27
Halloween!!! 28
Jack O' Lantern 29
A Night of Spooks 30
Trick or Treat 31
On the night of the witches 32
Halloween fun from a nearly-two perspective 33
Neither Trick nor Treat 34
Life Melody 35
Everybody likes Halloween 36
Halloween 37
Jack o'Lantern 38
The Halloween Thief 39
Trick or Treat 40
A Waiting Pint 41

Magic of Spirits 42
Photocamp 43
Binbag witch 44
The Broom 45
Sounds of Halloween 46
Devils Army 47
The dance of all hallows eve 48
Streets on Halloween.. 49
Poetry... 50

STREET POEMS... 51
Halloween Love 52
The Highlander's Halloween 53
Edinburgh Haiku 54
What a load of Bollocks 55
Camel Toe... 56
Halloween 57
Gorilla Man... 58
Halloween 59
Trick or Treat 60
Sleeping Advice.. 61
Hockey at Halloween 62
Christmas Rocks 63
It's not my Day Job 64
Here we are Scotland.. 65
Haunted Tree 66
Halloween Fools 67

SHORE POETS 68
The PoemCatcher's Spirit... 69
Hallowe'en Hansel 70
My Real Birthday 72
October End 2010 73
Hallowe'en 74
Community Garden Spirits... 75
Haiku on Halloween.. 76
Grassmarket 77

Bad Day	78
Oh -31st	79
Edge of the Village	80
Dookin'	81
Vessells	82
All Hallow's Eve	83
Next Winter	84
Adieu	85

ROYAL MILE SAMHUIN PARADE 86

Interfaith Halloween	87
Halloween – Queen	89
Cheers	90
Departure	91
Dooking for Pumpkins	93
Welcome	94
Autumn Falls	95
Ahmed's Poem	96
Samhuin	97
Untitled	98
Mile of Fire	99
Lo Siento	100
Apologies (from you to me)	101
Index of Authors	102

The Party

Hatters Halloween

Dressed up as my namesake
with friends and fine wine
Having a rare old time
with Darth and The Doctor
But remembering last year
with my once and future
My head may be here
But my heart is in Leeds

By Hatter

Cauldrons

When witches lie
the world will change
Spells Abound
For those they've slain

When witches lie
the world will change
Birth the new
in bed they've twain

When witches lie
the world will change
Thrice the pot
Stirs cauldron rain.

By PoemCatcher

Jenny's Halloween

This year at Halloween we were all very bad,
but it may be the most fun that we have ever had
Medusa and a Sith lord, and a kilted Devil.
Then some bloke we didn't invite, I think his name was Neville.
A Doctor Who, A cyber girl and a pretty princess.
I don't think I'll remember though
Maybe I should drink less.

By Jenny Whyte

Halloween

HALLOWEEN IS FUN

HALLOWEEN IS SILLY

HALLOWEN IS FULL OF BLACK KITTENS

By Flo

Hallow's Eve

All Hallow's Eve
to celebrate the dead,
to celebrate the lives they lived,
to enjoy life
to embrace death
not to fear it.
and to remember
to celebrate
those you have loved
and lost.

By Rachel Boddy

My Sh*t Halloween Poem!

Eight people sat around a decorated room

All scratching their head, in costume

Trying their best to write a poem that's witty

But all I offer is my Halloween poem, simple and Sh*tty!

By Mamil Inc

Halloween House

Orange purple black + sweet
squashing scary skeletons
Spider kittens and Batty cats,
meow
munchkin pumpkins

By Lisa Edgar

"Surprise"

Pumpkins, pizza, people, go
oooh – check it out – and
who are yooo? – bats and
blood – all kinds of scary
- give the vampire – a
bloody Mary!

By Cutty Sark

Binary Halloween Haiku

Poem Title: BINARY HALLOWEEN HAIKU

0010 1101 1001 0000 111
0100 0111 0011 0101 0101 1110 111
0010 1100 0000 111 0000

By Gavin Saxby

Paparazzi

Flashers

Ghoulish scots photocampers

Scare the souls from Burke and Hare's famous graveyard

When flashing the Royal Mile

By Jon

Forgot

Forgot the sweets for Halloween
So in my house I must stay unseen
When the children call
So I don't look mean.

By Anon

I've seen the PoemCatcher Error! Bookmark not defined.

It's nearly Halloween
& this is the first Poemcatcher I've ever seen
I took his picture,
On Flickr it will be a fixture
I hope it will be seen & Seen

By Brian Donovan

Fancy Dress

All Souls Night
The day that anyone can
Dress however they want.

Some try to scare
Others make an effort
to show that they care

Its a special day to me
For many reasons and memories
That others never will see.

By Maree Lucas

Make Believe on All Hallows Eve

Gleaming within strange lights
  I saw shimmering strange knights
Performing peculiar mystic rites
  Striking poses making odd sights
As they joined in ghostly delights
  In their All Hallow's Eve flights
We're all taken by the spirit of th nights
  That enraptures all it strikes

On all Hallows Eve
  Fantasies become true
  All changes all abouts you
Again we embrace make believe

By Phh Sykes

October Theifs

There's tapping at the window
There's footsteps on the floor
Howling in the darkness
Creaking in the door

Witches, bats and broomsticks
Fill the night time sky
Children scared to look up
On their night to sly

Illuminated pumpkins
with sharpened pumpkin teeth
shine from neighbours windows
to scare off little theifs

A song, a dance, a joke or two
to earn themselves a pound
As guisers fleece the neighbourhood
When halloween's around

By Keith Walker

Zombie Walk

Those who are going on a Zombie Walk
stumble and 'grrr' but do not talk
Maybe their grunts a poem will make
But until then many brains to take.

By E Robson

Images on Halloween

Poem Title: IMAGES ON HALLOWEEN

Images on Halloween
catch the mood
focus on horror.
Scar faces come alive
in a flash
Infra-red lens expose
the hidden
Blurred images and
imagination fly with
the Witches.

By Nicky L. Stones

Halloween

All Hallows Eve
When spirits walk the earth once more
Darkness engulfs the land
and fear overwhelms the masses
Until the break of dawn
When all is calm once more

By Sarah Adams

Halloween!!!

Halloween
A festival for witches
for monsters and gouls
and zombies held together by stitches

For sounds and screams
that will fill you with fright
SO hide in the shadows
and hope you make it through the night!

By Richie Gunn

Jack O' Lantern

Lights,

Peering out

I wonder

What he sees?

By Pam

A Night of Spooks

A night of spooks & scary bats
witches cauldrons & flying mats
Pumpkin Lanterns & Black Cats
Magic Wands & Pointy Hats
Children's faces shine with Glee
as they TRICK & TREAT with me.

By Lou Wood

Trick or Treat

        Kids in hockey masks

          Roam the streets

      Striking fear into all the

         People they meet,

      With the immortal words

          "trick or treat"

By Simon Sheehan

On the night of the witches

The night of the witches once more
The kids come knocking on the door
To scare, moan, groan like a ghost or ghoul
The more scary then the more cool
The requirements of the nights' only a mask
but never loose sight that its never a task

Have a Happy Halloween.

By Scott Armour

Halloween fun from a nearly-two perspective

You can dress up in costumes
of wizards and witches

You can 'scare' them with
dangly spiders and baddies

But they're oblivious to all of
the 'fun' and good wishes

And concentrate hard on
their food and their teddies!

By May Cruikshank

Neither Trick nor Treat

All Hallow's Eve
We've lost the real meaning
Now its all commercial,
Quite demeaning,
and not that special.

By Deb Ball

Life Melody

Halloween is always funny,
but it's also about life melody!
Enjoy your days with love and sympathy,
Even a penny can bring the world beauty

By Shawn Q

Everybody likes Halloween

Thrill is for the horror movies

Halloween is lots of funny things
People like Halloween,
because we like fun things
We enjoy the parties,
While children love the candies,
Witches on the street,
mouths filled with sweet.
We like Halloween,
Because everybody win

By Wang Xuan

Halloween

Halloween frightening scenes
      Scary faces make you scream
      Haunted Houses, witches ghouls
      Or are they only silly fools
      Getting dressed up every year
      just to in still lots of fear

By RoseMarie Armour

Jack o'Lantern

All Hallows Eve
is not a nice time of year
if you happen to be
a pumpkin

How would you like it
if they sliced off the top of your head,
scooped out your brains
and carved up your face
so your own mother wouldn't
recognise you?

Then you're left to roast
slowly, from the inside out,
in the heat of one small candle.

Never mind, we'll have the last laugh.
Come Saints Day,
you'll be dining on pumpkin pie,
baked pumpkin, pumpkin soup,
pumpkin kebabs.

By Fiona Carmichael

The Halloween Thief

HALLOWEEN DRAWS OUT ALL SORTS OF FOLK
GHOULS, SPIDERS, GHOSTS AND FIENDISH GNOMES
- EVEN MEN WHO STEAL YOUR POEMS!

BY Jurgen Van Wessel

Trick or Treat

My sweet child
with golden curls,
and eyes of blue
why don't I
dress you
as a witch
with a pointy hat

Would you like that?
I'll send you out into the dark
through the park
to knock on doors
to demand sweets and treats
won't that be fun.
my little one.

By Pam Thorburn

A Waiting Pint

TIME PASSES

A Room with no windows
A Pint waits

FAR AWAY.

By Paul Aitken

Magic of Spirits

The wind howls,
 making a waterfall of shimmering
red, yellow & orange leaves,
falling of the sleeping trees.

The evil pumpkins grin showing off their sparkly teeth.
It is that time of year again,
when the magic of spirits are upon us.

By Aroosha Laghaee

Photocamp

Poem Title: Photocamp

Today I went to photocamp
To learn about photography
~~Tomorrow we're going into Edinburgh~~ Tomorrow we're taking photos in Edinburgh
Let's hope the weather is sunny and not damp.

By Neil Robinson

Binbag witch

Drink a toast to a bedsheet ghost,
Give some sweets to a Franken – teen
A mummy with rags or witch wearing binbags,
because tonight is Halloween

By John McCarthey

The Broom

INSPIRATION RUNNING DAY
I TOOK A PHOTO OF THIS GUY
HE TOOK HIS FUNNY LOOKING BROOM
AND CARRIED IT AROUND THIS ROOM
IN SEARCH OF DITTIES
MAYBE WITTIES
HIS BROOM IT TURNED INTO A NET
TO CAPTURE WHAT IN PRINT TO SET.

By Donald Tainsh

Sounds of Halloween

Yum~ Yum~
Pumpkin.

Whoo~ Whoo~
Wolfman.

Shhhh~Shhhh~
Spirit.

"Trick or Treat"
Oh! No! The children are coming.

By Evelyn

Devils Army

Halloween Halloween Halloween!!!
Oh Great what a day,
Feels Like Devils army Landed on earth!!
 But I feel like a new recruit in it.

A little girl passing by scared me
think my make up didn't worked
well!!!

Halloween Halloween, what a Grand
Day!!

By Jaggi Lotey

The dance of all hallows eve

Halloween is no different
For shadows are always in my head,
Creeping, haunting images
Never allowed to rest.

Halloween is no different
for I always wear a mask
I might be kind not horror,
But shows little of within in.

Halloween is not different
For the world is always pretence
The spirits of the dead may rise
But am always dead.

By Laura

Streets on Halloween

Wondering the streets on Halloween
Oh what sights to be seen
From Gorgie to Morningside
and in between,
Many a pumpkin glow has been seen.

From my sanctuary of Loopy Lornas
with a hot cup of tea and a scone,
As the sun starts to fade
and darkness begins to fall
Witches, goblins, ghosts and ghouls
take to the streets of the toon

In trepidation I venture back out,
Trick or treat:
most of them shout out loud :0)
I smile; then suddenly
I hear a howl, that makes me quiver,

Watch out the night is not all it seems on Halloween!!

By Miss Blossom.

Poetry

Poetry
does not come easily
words that do not rhyme
wash over my mind
and even more
tricky is finding
an ending
which doesn't.

By John

STREET POEMS

Halloween Love

Being couped up all year,
Halloween is finally here
Us ghosts will appear
and they shall be near
to those once so dear
But many fear
The wind in their ears
That brings them to tears,
But listen here,
Listen clear,
Our love is sincere

By Carlairi

The Highlander's Halloween

An Edinburgh Halloween
with Ghosts and Ghouls & a shrieking scream.
Take a walk through the cemetery
The Mackenzie ghost is frightfully scary
A vampire walking down the street
Accompanied by some zombie feet.
A Scottish Bagpipe screams and wails
A touring guide tells ghostly tales
Edinburgh Halloween
Will make you shriek, will make you scream.

By Melissa Penner

Edinburgh Haiku

Daylight ends just now
Sunset falls on Auld Reekie
Edinburgh lives on

By Joss Smiles

What a load of Bollocks

There was a young witch called Vonnie
who was exceptionally bonny
When Halloween came
Her broom was aflame
and her cat, she had to sell for some money.

By Vonnie The Witch

Camel Toe

I'm a pumpkin
and I have a camel toe,
I also have a friend who's a ghost
One day , he stole my post!

By Flora Henry

Halloween

Witches, Ghouls & floating stools
are the things that scare me most.
Other men try to act tough
Inflate their chests and boast,

> "I'm not afraid of Halloween
> stools that float or witches that scream"

But all this showy bravery
I knew to be a lie
because the things that make
a grown man cry
is a smelly stool
Which can bring tears to the eye.

By Gary Quinn

Gorilla Man

Poem Title: Gorilla Man

There once was a man who played drums,
Who happened to look for some chums,
We wrote him a poem,
Te minute we saw 'im,
As we happily filled up our tums.

By Pam, Laura-Ann & Cathy

Halloween

Happy Halloween! It's
All Hallows Eve,
Lucifer!
Larks! (ie like Hitchcock's The Birds) (it's scary)
Oh, it's very scary!
Warlocks and witches, cats and bats
Eek!
Eek!
Nooooooo....!

By Fiona Beggs

Trick or Treat

Poem Title: Trick or Treat

Halloween is coming and the pumpkin's getting fat!
Please put some candy in the witches hat.
If you haven't got candy then penny's will do.
If you haven't got penny's then goblins haunt you!!

By Lara Green & Kristin Lamb

Sleeping Advice

Goodnight my dear
and sweet repose
lie on you back
and you won't squash your nose.

By Mighty Quinn

Hockey at Halloween

Poem Title: HOCKEY AT HALLOWEEN

In the dark depth of the locker room
The players ply their trade
The bunnies gather round
Like the zombie bride to the zombie groom

The Steeler take the ice
The bunnies stand and pout
The crowd it gathers motion
Edinburgh at Halloween is
        fantastic and nice
           xx

By Custard Puckbunnies

Christmas Rocks

Costumes and ghosts,
pubs and beer,
screaming and shouting,
Why am I here?

Oh, I forgot, it's Halloween
I think that's just mean.
I'd rather have Chritsmas
and that's the whole business

Singing the carols
Hark the harolds
the saviour from above
that's what I love.

By Lea

It's not my Day Job

My tasks at night
are not your usual type
with targets of fright
and a kill with a hype.

The dead are my friends
when they're in my sights
say "goodbye" fair zombie
the hunter says "goodnight"

By Tom Piddock "ZOMBIE HUNTER"

Here we are Scotland

Poem Title: Here we Are, Scotland

Scotland, Scotland, Scotland
I love the weather
I love the places
Halloween, Helloween, Hellonken
I love the dressing
I love the style
Be enjoy & Happy in Halloween Day.

By Nancy

Haunted Tree

Poem Title: HAUNTED TREE

The tree has no more leafs,
and no more fruits,
in the night it's very dark
and the moon howls over the haunted tree,
the bats hang upside down on the tree, and fly away in the night,
and there the haunted tree stands, alone in the middle of ~~nowhere~~ of the night

By Emily (10 yrs old)

Halloween Fools

Poem Title: Halloween fools.

Halloween, Halloween, Halloween
People dressed here and there
they are so crazy to make
them self looks like fools,
when they ~~he~~ think
halloween is cool,
such.

HALLOWEEN FOOLS

9 yrs old

By Ashleigh (9yrs old)

Shore Poets

The PoemCatcher's Spirit

The poemcatcher's
Spirit has got me again
With a fear of ghost writers
I pick up my pen

When Grass Market Ghouls
attack me and then
I jump back afeared
of things that are clearly
beyond my own ken
That are spooky and Weird

By Simon Maclaren

Hallowe'en Hansel

A boannie nicht for castin kale:
a fat mön vaegin owre Sannis,
a hale gadderie o laads an lasses.

A spree i der blöd,
laads loupit dykes
purled kale-stocks
iggit een anidder on
ripe da rigs
hunse fur hens
whit a stramash
an dan da dash
tae a porch door
lift da sneck
ball in da booty
rin like da mellishon
dunna look back.

But dee an me
pooskered wi da bassel
fell ahint ta draa breath,
taste wir first smoorikin.
But aa I can mind is da mön
gaffin at me in mi cöttikins
wis ahint a uncan barn
an dy blate Hansel
anunder a kendlin o starns.

Translations:

hansel: gift to mark an inaugural occasion; boannie: bonnie; castin kale: the childhood.Hallowe'en tradition of stealing croft produce such as cabbages and throwing them in doorways; mön: moon; vaegin: wandering, travelling; owre: over; hale: whole; gadderie: gathering; spree: jollification; i: in; der: their; blöd: blood; loupit: jumped; purled: poked about; kale-stocks: cabbages; iggit on: incited; een anidder: one another; to ripe: to harvest; rigs: fields; hunse: rummage; fur: for; whit: what; stramash: commotion; dan: then; tae: to; sneck: latch; ball: throw; rin: run; the mellishon: the devil; dunna: do not; dee: you (familiar); pooskered: exhausted; wi: with; bassel: struggle; ahint: behind; draa: draw; wir: our; smoorikin: kiss; aa: all; mind: remember; gaffin: laughing; mi: my; cöttikins: ankle socks; wis: us; uncan: unfamiliar; dy: your (familiar); blate: shy; anunder: under; kendlin: live coals; starns: stars

By Christine De Luca

My Real Birthday

I spent last year stuck
In a club full of pirates
Empty, some kind of competition.
I thought that I was a vampire
Full of pride,
They're so vain, but if they
Could swallow those mirrors
Maybe they'd be able to
Reflect a little,
But those guys just bleed
Everyone dry

By Criss Roden

October End 2010

We all gather at this time of year,
Not to frighten or perturbe;
but make contact with you -
Now we're on the other side.

    "What side," you ask?

The other side of this same world -
another view of your reality.
Same home, fields, same gardens, rooms
same pets, same friends -
viewed from beyond, not seen,
Watching you from the shadow, but no threat

By Jane Mary Wilde

Hallowe'en

Hallowe'en
Hallowed even though
It's children sticky
with sweets,
high on
sugar,
dayglo.
plastic clad
hungry for
more.

Annoymous

Community Garden Spirits

Free at last
I travel North
In time for lunch
Its Halloween
The garden's full
Children in fancydress
Provide their parents
with the rationale
for a party
rationales
A garden party
Ghosts and ghouls, Dragons
and demons
Pumkin lanterns
Mulled wine
Chilled beer
Community Garden Spirits Soar

By Anne Miller

Haiku on Halloween

A Royal Mile
of newly painted Ghouls
- a close call for
all souls of St Giles

By Gordon Peters

Grassmarket

In the Grassmarket
there's a bloody basket
full of heads
and things not dead
In the Royal Mile
Ghouls smile
There's witches hats
and spooky bats
In the half light
Werewolfs bite

By Simon Maclaren

Bad Day

Black dog day in greasy eddy's
trapped together and then apart.
Bitter essay repeated, the flotsam
clogged and stinking
without escape and cleansing tide
We drown

Anonymous

Oh -31st

Axe through the head.
Blood everywhere.
I found the reactions strange.
Ghoulish mendicants at the door
overdue interest in fruit
Busier night than usual
Supermarket seems different
All the clocks are wrong
I'm going back to my own country
its really scary here.

By Alan Condy

Edge of the Village

Poem Title: EDGE OF THE VILLAGE

Bold under old sheets
amassing plunder
in our mothers' shopping bags
we toured the scatter of village streets.
Neighbours waited patiently
as we raised our pluck
to stumble through a tune or rhyme,
then showered us with apples, nuts and penny chews.

But there was one house
where we'd never call,
a place of looming shadows,
where the rhymes died in our throats.
Behind its shuttered windows we could sense
the real Haloween stirring in the dark.

By Ian McDonough

Dookin'

Russett, Bramley
Granny Smith
Adam thought Eve
Was takin' the piss
Ye spoke tae a serpent?
Conversed wi' a snake?
And now a'm tae eat
That wee tart that you've baked?
But ye ken whit HE tellt ye?
Ye ken it's forbidden
Tae go dookin' fe apples
In the garden o' Eden.

By Hugh Dailly

Vessells

Small while empty boats
wait calmly on the sea
I am full of them.

By Thomlaycoch

All Hallow's Eve

Dark and Wet the
Clock chimes in a
Whirl of sound
While guizers stalk the
Street of fear and
Dreading --------- Wistful sigh...

By Alan

Next Winter

Above the roofs the round
moon forgot the dark
shone, silvery with a blue rim.
Watched the creatures of the
night going about their day routines.
Asked them to dance in her circle
to enter the coming winter.

By Ana Maguire

Adieu

Scary night of fun
We bid the summer goodbye
We enjoy Samheinn

Anonymous

Royal Mile Samhuin Parade

Interfaith Halloween

"Can I have a hot chocolate
Without a conversation about Jesus please?
(I'm cold and the conflict of our beliefs
will neither
warm my heart
nor toes)"

    asked the bosomly maiden
    painted in ivy,
    earthyness exuding,
    bucket in hand.

The collectors meet.

    One: 'All Heart'
    Gathering "Lost Souls"
    Of those poor people who
    Do not understand
    "HIS" Love

    The Other: all bosom
    Gathering lures and leers
    Enticing and delighting her agenda
    For money

The offertory hymm looks different
when sung to drums of darkness.
Outdoor ritual fires the giving

And I consider...
Which opens my wallet
With more ease and grace?
The buxom playfulness or guilty hymn?
And while these two shall never meet
Bosom to Bosom or Heart to Heart
How different is the call?

By PoemCatcher

Halloween - Queen

I like pumpkins
I like muffins
when I get that I feel like a Queen
and that's for me Halloween

By Gilles & Claire

Cheers

Poem Title: CHEERS

SAMHUINN REFECIT ET RECREAT
EAS PARTES QUAS BELTANE

SAMHUINN
REFECIT ET
RECREAT
EAS PARTES
QUAS
BELTANE
NON ATTINGUNT

By Mandy

Departure

Poem Title: Departure

fire shines through hallows eve
beckoning, the spirits leave

pounding drums braves the night
to see the demons out of sight
our kindreds gather in
their masses, to
celebrate how summer passes

I'm taking a guess at the final version below:

Pounding drums brave the night
to see the demons out of sight

Our kindreds gather in their masses
To celebrate hour summer passes

By Nick and Tom

Dooking for Pumpkins

Poem Title: Dooking for pumpkins,

Still reflection
a liquid pane
but not apple bobbing
pumpkins
orange as a carrot
orange as an orange
and too big.
Just.

By Gwen f.m.

Welcome

As I was standing in the dark
My mind got just a little spark
that turned in a fire
It burnt my deep and serious thoughts
So I can laugh about the cold
of scary winters love

By Constant Dancer

Autumn Falls

Poem Title: ~~Autumn Falls~~

~~Autumn falls~~
~~Edinburgh, but~~

A Black cat crossed
my path tonight
as I rode past the Loch
A thousand ravens and
many more screamed
riotous in the ~~dark~~ trees
Darkness
Night falls,
fives light.

Anonymous

Ahmed's Poem

Poem Title: ليلة الهلاوين

هذي الهلاوين ياهدرتي ويشهدو متمدها
وأسماء الطيبة ياحبيب شارتها
يا واحد ما كل خلقه تلتفت صوبها
تسعد هل الديك واهل الربع مردها
أحمد شفلوح لطفان ١٠/١٠/٣٠ م
مع تحيات /
يحيى سعيد آل شطوط

By Ahmed

Samhuin

Samhuin, fire, hope, joy
A crowd full of excitement
Winter king will rule.

By Amy

Untitled

You asked for a poem
on the night of Halloween
And I'm there waiting
for inspiration to begin
So, darling, that's the best I'll do
But you'll still know I wrote this for you.

By Camilla

Mile of Fire

Its's all Hallow's eve

Spirits high and ghosts around

Fire burns the night

By Julia Q and Danielle S

Lo Siento

Poem Title: Lo Siento

Lo siento que me vaya
prendiendo toda una batalla
de viejos sentimientos, violentos,
remordimientos.

Lo siento que no vaya a acompañarte
mas que durante
esta pequeña parte

Lo siento que me voy, &
y no te doy mas que hoy
a mi también me duele

By Lara Luna Bartley

Apologies (from you to me)

Dear PoemCatcher

Sorry for the handwriting that you could not read, and sorry for the metric rhythm that you could not follow and sorry for not giving the poem a title, and thank you, so much for giving it a title for me (why didn't you just ask?, I would have done it happily) and I forgive you for typing up the most poignant moment of the poem with the wrong word. (I promise to write neater next time).

Oh, don't worry about the auto-capitalising of all the little-letters I so carefully choose to punctuate. I understand the nuances of word-processing in a hurry.

Lastly sorry for not seeing my own brilliance. I wrote a great poem and then dissed it myself. I've had time to reflect and I'm pretty chuffed that I could write such an amazing poem so spontaneously. I really like my own poem. I was brilliant.

I promise to write some more

With Love
The Aspirational Poet

Index of Authors

Ahmed, 96
Alan, 79, 83
Amy, 97
Ana, 84
Anne, 75
Anon, 20
Aroosha, 43
Ashleigh, 67
Brian, 21
Camilla, 98
Carlairi, 52
Christine, 71
Constant Dancer, 94
Criss, 72
Custard Puckbunnies, 62
Cutty Sark, 16
Danielle, 99
Deb, 34
Donald, 46
E Robson, 25
Emily, 66
Evelyn, 47
Fiona, 39, 59
Flo, 12
Flora, 56
Gary, 57
Gavin, 17
Gilles & Claire, 89
Gordon, 76
Gwen, 93
Hatter, 9

Hugh, 81
Ian, 80
Jaggi, 48
Jane Mary, 73
Jenny, 11
John, 45, 51
Jon, 19
Joss, 54
Julia, 99
Jurgen, 40
Keith, 24
Kristin, 60
Lara, 60
Lara Luna, 100
Laura, 49, 58
Lea, 63
Lisa, 15
Lou, 30
Mamil Inc, 14
Mandy, 90
Maree, 22
May, 33
Melissa, 53
Mighty Quinn, 61
Miss Blossom, 50
Nancy, 65
Neil, 44
Nick, 92
Nicky L., 26
Pam, 29, 41, 58
Paul, 42

102

Phh Sykes, 23
PoemCatcher, 10, 37, 88
Rachel, 13
Richie, 28
RoseMarie, 38
Sarah, 27
Scott, 32
Shawn Q, 35
Simon, 31, 69, 77
Thomlaycoch, 82
Tom, 92
Vonnie The Witch, 55
Wang, 36

Other PoemCatcher Books

QUAKE Built from Nothing
Made in 4 days, begging for poems on the pavements of St Andrew's, as an unofficial one-man fringe event for StAnza poetry festival 2010

BALLS from the Queue (Game, Set and Match
A trilogy of tennis poems captured at Wimbledon 2010 in the infamous queue for centre court tickets.

FUNGUS Poems
Mushroom and fungal poetry written by the world's leading scientists at the 9th international Mycology Conference in Edinburgh

SALTY Poems from the Sea
Capturing the delights of a British Summer festival in the Seaside town of North Berwick – during "Fringe By The Sea 2010" (This book includes a self-guided historic walking tour)

FANTASTIC FIREWORKS
Sparkling, explosive poetry from the Edinburgh festival Fireworks display.

www.ingramcontent.com/pod-product-compliance
Lightning Source LLC
Chambersburg PA
CBHW051455290426
44109CB00016B/1771